# *The*
# BOUNDLESS
# COMPASSION
# *Journal*

"We often need assistance in taking that first step on any new journey. With *The Boundless Compassion Journal*, Joyce Rupp provides that helping hand for those already familiar with journaling or living a compassion-centered life as well as those embracing both for the first time. Rupp gently encourages us to place on paper the words, colors, and shapes of our own boundless experiences of compassion."

**Rick Klein**
Boundless Compassion program facilitator

"In this companion to *Boundless Compassion*, Joyce Rupp guides us through the transformative practice of journaling. Along the way, she shows us how to delve into our stories in a compassionate journey of self-care, courage, peace, purpose, and growth. Intimate and inspiring, *The Boundless Compassion Journal* offers poetry, prayers, and prompts that invite us to explore our experiences and nourish compassionate living."

**Wendy Mospan**
Boundless Compassion program facilitator and Facebook page moderator

"As a Boundless Compassion program facilitator and journal writer, I am excited to see how Joyce Rupp has reimagined the original *Boundless Compassion* in this new journal format. Readers can find space to release memories, burdens, and joys to the open page. I recognize newly distilled insights and, in the quotations that make clear that the focus on compassion stretches into many disciplines, the names of now-familiar authors. Take up the challenge of listening compassionately to your own story and experience fresh 'aha!' moments."

**Mary Dean Pfahler, S.N.D.**
Boundless Compassion program facilitator

"Joyce Rupp engages us with her poetry, personal experiences, and rich quotes to draw us more deeply into understanding and practicing a compassionate presence in *The Boundless Compassion Journal*. As a Boundless Compassion program facilitator of book studies and retreats, I find this journal a truly valuable companion to use for individual reflection and group sharing."

**Bobbi Bussan, O.S.B.**
Director of the Benet House Retreat Center
Boundless Compassion program facilitator

# The
# BOUNDLESS
# COMPASSION
# Journal

Creating a Way of Life

# JOYCE RUPP

SORIN BOOKS  Notre Dame, IN

© 2021 by Joyce Rupp

All rights reserved. No part of this book may be used or reproduced in any manner whatsoever, except in the case of reprints in the context of reviews, without written permission from Sorin Books®, P.O. Box 428, Notre Dame, IN 46556-0428, 1-800-282-1865.

www.sorinbooks.com

Paperback: ISBN-13 978-1-932057-24-9

Cover image © 2018 Alicia Brown/Stocksy.

Cover and text design by Brianna Dombo.

Printed and bound in the United States of America.

# THE STRENGTH OF COMPASSION

Douglas firs, rising tall, extensive roots,
stout-hearted trunks, strong branches,
marked with scars from severe storms,
scorched bare from lightning strikes,
pocked with the unwanted entrance
of hungry creatures constantly feeding—
vulnerable, like our own humanity.

How much these magnificent trees
teach me about my exposed life,
the endless, spiraling current of it—
dark storms followed by cobalt skies,
hurt and healing, loss and then gain,
damage from disregarded self-care,
inner resilience and recovery.

Like the timbered friends standing tall,
I want to stand that way in compassion,
rely on the strength of love within me,
embrace what I would much rather avoid,
provide for those seeking nurturance,
and join my soul in silent communion
with the Great Love sustaining all
in the dense forest we know as our life.

~ *Joyce Rupp*

# CONTENTS

# $\mathscr{I}$NTRODUCTION

To stay with experiences of suffering and loss until we
coax the deeper meaning and beauty from them is a
challenge that growing in compassion asks of us.

~ Catherine T. Nerney, *The Compassion Connection*[1]

Turning toward what is difficult, listening to what clamors for
attention—I used to sidestep those very things that deserved my
consideration. Compassion has taught me to enter what I would
rather circumvent. When I attend and move through aspects of my
own story, it readies me to listen to other people's stories. Meaningful perceptions surface when I pause for reflection and follow
this by putting pen to paper. Sometimes a connection between the
current moment and the distant past arises. Almost always a clearer
awareness of what has recently taken place appears on the pages.
Although I have been keeping a journal for more than fifty years,
I'm still surprised at how the process of journaling fosters personal
transformation. I never cease being grateful for the unexpected
reassurance, for the stretching and meaningful insights that hearken
to me.

How did it all begin? I go back to an event when my inner
life contained quite a bit of fogginess. Life was moving along OK

externally, although I was unsure as to whom I was becoming. Acute sorrow joined that emotional atmosphere on the day I received word of my twenty-three-year–old brother, David, drowning in a fishing accident. I was twenty-five at the time and became lost in a swirl of sadness. I didn't know how to absorb the devastating news. This occurred in the mid-1960s while I was living with three other members of my religious community, each of whom was quite a bit older and reticent regarding conversation about their interior life (a commonality during that era). I felt I had no one with whom to explore the anguish that embedded itself like a rock within me.

At the time my brother died, I had been reading a book by Fr. Edward Farrell. I've forgotten the title of the book but not the content. It influenced my inner life significantly. Farrell described a practice called "keeping a journal," a process new to me. I felt drawn to his suggestion that this method of reflection could be valuable for spiritual growth. I now marvel how it was that I made the decision to go every day to the nearby woods after teaching school. With a notebook and Bible, I sat down under a tree. I really did not know how to "journal," but I instinctively fell into it by choosing and reflecting on a biblical passage, followed by writing a prayer. After a few months, that process grew into also addressing my grief and loneliness. In doing so, I learned how to companion myself by being attentive and listening. Thus began my initiation into a spiritual practice that continues to this day.

Those two "under the tree" years opened my inner being. Reflection and writing held me together emotionally, instilled courage to face what was difficult, and brought a semblance of peace. Eventually, journal-keeping led to finding meaning, inspiration, and a clearer purpose for a life of service focused on compassion. I cannot imagine my interior life maturing without including this spiritual practice.

## USING THIS JOURNAL

Keeping a journal includes more than exploring and recording experiences of suffering. In journaling, we delve into any and all aspects regarding our lives. I encourage you to approach this specific journal as a way to discover what can assist your ongoing growth in compassionate living. In doing so, you will be exploring various layers of your life, such as your memories, relationships, experiences, and emotions. I hope you find support for your exploration through this journal, along with deeper meaning and further insight into your spirituality.

The journal follows closely the content and focus of the *Boundless Compassion* book, with the prompts (suggestions) for reflection similar to those found in the book at the end of each Day. A few of the prompts have been adapted or changed to more readily relate to the content of the book.

Instead of considering the prompts as "lead-ins for reflection," I prefer to think of them as *assistants for integration*. Too often the material in a book exists as a source of information without connecting this information to how we go about our lives. The process of journaling encourages the content to become rooted within us, where it then grows and affects our lived experience, directly influencing thoughts, feelings, words, and deeds. This journal aims to assist you in activating and strengthening compassion as a way of life.

Sometimes more than one integrative prompt is presented for each Day. Choose the one to which you are most drawn. This especially refers to Day Seven of each Week. You will always have more than one choice on Day Seven by which to review the Week's content. There will be times, too, when no prompt appeals to you. If this happens, follow your inclination and reflect on what most stirs within you regarding the topic of a Day and the review of a Week.

You could also use the quote accompanying the Day as your prompt. These quotes are in addition to the ones found in the

*Boundless Compassion* book. Each quote was chosen in order to deepen and enhance the topic. At times, you may find this selection more appealing and enriching than the prompt. Either way, I encourage you to pause and hold the quote in your mind and heart for a while. Savor the message until you taste its relevance for your life.

You will notice that the pages are blank rather than lined. This allows for freedom to sketch or draw instead of writing, if that is your preferred style of registering what surfaces from your deeper self. Only you know what might be the best approach for recording your ponderings. Sometimes you may want to alternate between these two methods.

Listening and sharing with others who are also using this journal provides an additional support for writing and increased integration. The resource "Weekly Reflection with Groups" is included in the back of this journal to aid those who meet for group conversation each week.

The journal you are now holding in your hands has arrived due to Colleen Shephard, one of our certified facilitators of the *Boundless Compassion* program. At the workshop in California where Colleen trained, she suggested that I design a journal to accompany the book. I thought her request to be excellent but set it aside due to numerous other commitments. A year later, when I gathered for retreat with some of the facilitators, Colleen again encouraged the creation of the journal. I finally got the message, and here it is, ready for you to use.

As you prepare to make your entry into *The Boundless Compassion Journal*, my hope for its effect and influence on your life is expressed in the words of the poet, Rabindranath Tagore: "The emancipation of our physical nature is in attaining health, of our social being in attaining goodness, and of our self in attaining love . . . the extinction of selfishness. This is the function of love, and it does not lead to darkness but to illumination."[2]

May the *illumination* you receive from using this journal light your way and encourage you to live more fully the treasure of compassion dwelling within you.

# COMPASSION AS A WAY OF LIFE

## A RIGHT TO BE HERE

My own space, my own solitude,
my own this, my own that—
tribalism grown through centuries
wants to protect, claim, shut out.

Here by the river with its quiet flow
another human being arrives,
parks his car next to mine,
and the old brain in me leaps up,
shouts silently, "Stay away from me!"

My newer brain intervenes,
"He has every right to be here,
to make breakfast by the river,
to enjoy the peaceful beauty
same as I am doing now."

He takes the bag of charcoal,
piles the briquettes on the grill,
and I pull back my defenses,
glad now that he, too, wants
to take in the breath of creation.

"We are one," I say to those I teach.
Now I practice it, take it in, make it mine.
Oops, there I go again, "mine"—
the ancient brain claiming things,
caught in the old tribal language
that refuses to go away.

*~ Joyce Rupp*

# WEEK 1, DAY 1

## AWARENESS, ATTITUDE, ACTION

### INTEGRATION

Of the three components of compassion—awareness, attitude, action—which do you find most difficult to live? What makes this challenging for you? How might you approach this so it becomes less difficult?

Compassion impels us to work tirelessly to alleviate the suffering of our fellow creatures, to dethrone ourselves from the center of our world and put another there, and to honor the inviolable sanctity of every single human being, treating everybody, without exception, with absolute justice, equity and respect.

~ The Charter for Compassion[1]

## WEEK 1, DAY 2

# THE SEEDS OF COMPASSION

INTEGRATION

Which of the four seeds of compassion—nonjudgment, nonviolence, forgiveness, mindfulness—could most use some tending in the garden of your heart? List some ways you can nurture this seed. What might the divine Gardener say to you about this?

The seeds sown in our lives are, in reality, seeds of our potential. They are sparks of the divine. They must take root in the earthiness of our lives and grow.

~ Macrina Wiederkehr, *The Song of the Seed* [2]

## **WEEK 1, DAY 3**

# BEHIND EVERY SCAR, A STORY

INTEGRATION

Call to mind someone whom you judge disapprovingly or someone whom you wish to change in order to meet your criteria. Imagine you are standing behind that person's back, looking out through his or her eyes. What do you see? How might this person be hurting?

This ability to have empathy for difference, to be open to diversity, to work hard at thinking about how other people may differ from you is a key step on the road to compassion—and it's not always easy.

~ Paul Gilbert, *The Compassionate Mind* [3]

## WEEK 1, DAY 4

# RESPONDING NONVIOLENTLY

INTEGRATION

Look to your past. When did the instinctual part of your brain take over and lead you to respond with some form of violence in thought, word, gesture, silence, or action? Have a conversation with this part of your brain to understand what urged you to respond in the manner that you did.

When you say something that doesn't conform to or support my world view, then I find some way of killing you off. . . . Not with a gas chamber or a bullet, but with a phrase of dismissal or diminution, to render you irrelevant to my life.

~ Parker J. Palmer, *An Undivided Life*[4]

# WEEK 1, DAY 5

## FORGIVENESS IS A JOURNEY

INTEGRATION

What do you believe about forgiveness? What would you say to someone who asks you what is needed in order to forgive? Write to the part of your heart that continues to carry unforgiveness.

So we will be able to forgive if we can place ourselves in another's shoes; if we are less concerned with judgment, and more with understanding; if we are humble enough to give up being the patron of justice, and flexible enough to let go of past hurts and resentments. To learn how to forgive leads us to a radical transformation of our personality.

~ Piero Ferrucci, *The Power of Kindness*[5]

## WEEK 1, DAY 6

## STAYING AWAKE

INTEGRATION

Recall an experience where being mindful helped you to respond to another's suffering. How did being mindful make a difference? What usually keeps you from being attentive to suffering? How might you practice becoming more aware?

Attentiveness focuses energy; it establishes a sense of mutuality, intimacy, presence to the other. Attentiveness enables us to get out of the way in order to receive the other.

~ Elaine Prevallet, *Toward a Spirituality for Global Justice*[6]

## WEEK 1, DAY 7

## REVIEW

INTEGRATION

Choose any or all of the following as a way to review Week One:

- What three aspects of "Compassion as a Way of Life" were of greatest significance to you this past Week?

- How did the reflections of this Week connect with your experience of the spiritual life?

- As this first Week ends, what are your thoughts and feelings regarding the activation of compassion in your life?

- Draw your "Tree of Compassion."
  - Roots: Your life experiences that provided a strong foundation for the practice of compassion.
  - Trunk: Personal qualities and characteristics that enable you to be a conduit of compassion.
  - Branches: Situations and circumstances that challenge you to reach out with compassion.
  - Leaves: How you have received compassion from others.
  - Fruit: Specific ways you have offered compassion to yourself and others.

- As you look back over the Week, were there moments or situations that awakened your compassion? Describe how they did so.

- Which Day's reflection challenged you the most? Why?

Meandering through the forest, I pause and stand beneath a massive oak tree, glimpsing the history of its long journey: the forest floor embracing one lone acorn, wrapping hope around the contained strength, moisture slowly seeping into it and glints of sunlight encouraging the secreted life inside to grow. Standing in the forest with humbled awe, I turn inward to wonder what has grown in my life—from what source has my tree of compassion seeded, rooted, and given itself to growth?

~ Joyce Rupp (Personal Journal)

# NEWLY OPENED SPACE

Spirit of Love, you faithfully stir my heart
and inspire my mind to think compassionately.
I thank you for continuing to lead me toward
a desire to be a more loving human being.

I pray to activate the following intentions:

Be aware of what tries to lessen my kindness.
Choose to develop a compassionate presence
by widening my mind and expanding my heart.
Allow false thoughts and pretenses to crumble.
Stretch past each unkind judgment that arises.
Become attuned to where my resistance resides.
Let go of harmful attitudes and useless fears
and wash away excessive immersion in myself.

Spirit of Love, keep gently persuading me to grow
so ever more of who I am reflects your love.
Like charcoal clouds departing the morning sky,
let whatever fails to reflect compassion drift away
until my life reveals a wide sky of loving-kindness.

*~ Joyce Rupp*

# WELCOMING OURSELVES

## COMPASSION FOR SELF

The more we can trust the loving inside ourselves,
the more we can connect with others from a place
of wholeness, spontaneity, and authentic care.

~ Tara Brach, *Radical Compassion*[1]

To be there for myself today,
for no other reason
than to be there in full attention,
listening with kindness—
this, after constantly emptying out,
giving generously with no holding back.
Finally, a resting place in the home
of my heart, where I bow humbly
to the wonder of my soul, welcoming
the fountain of love and goodness.

And what do I hear affirmed
when all the pulls and pushes
are exhausted and finally set aside?
A faint whisper slowly emanates
from the far inward chamber,
revealing the truth I have known
and set aside time and again:
I am worthy of my attention.
I, too, have a need to be heard,
to be appreciated, to be loved.

~ *Joyce Rupp*

## WEEK 2, DAY 1

## BREATHING IN AND OUT

INTEGRATION

What areas of your life need more care? How might you go about doing this (layer and balance activities, release self-critical thoughts and feelings, identify and discard negative mindsets, fortify positive qualities, etc.)?

In preparing a self-care program for myself that touched all the bases, I needed to ensure that I had quiet time to renew, reflect, adjust, be in touch with myself, and simply breathe rather than taking in air and life in gulps.

~ Robert J. Wicks, *Night Call*[2]

## WEEK 2, DAY 2

## THE SELF-COMPASSION OF JESUS

INTEGRATION

Which of the self-compassion experiences of Jesus especially relates to your life experience? If you were to write a letter to Jesus about self-compassion, what would that letter contain?

How can anyone be compassionate toward her neighbor who is not compassionate toward herself? That is why Jesus says, "Be compassionate!" He wants our
compassion to begin at home, he wants us to be compassionate toward our own
body and soul.

~ Matthew Fox, *Meditations with Meister Eckhart*[3]

## WEEK 2, DAY 3

# APPRENTICE YOURSELF TO YOURSELF

INTEGRATION

How do the characteristics of your family history and personality influence your approach to self-compassion? Which is most supportive? Least supportive?

Hearing others all the way to their own story requires that we continue plunging courageously into our own. We can only accompany people as far as we ourselves have gone. We can only bear witness to the joy and suffering that we ourselves can both allow and feel all the way through.

~ Diane M. Millis, *Re-Creating a Life*[4]

## WEEK 2, DAY 4

# THE PROBLEM WITH PERFECTION

INTEGRATION

Can you accept your less-than-perfect self? Have a conversation with the part of yourself that you least like. What do you tell that part?

Perfectionism is the belief that if we live perfect, look perfect, and act perfect, we can minimize or avoid the pain of blame, judgment, and shame. . . . When we become more loving and compassionate with ourselves and we begin to practice shame resilience, we can embrace our imperfections.

~ Brené Brown, *The Gifts of Imperfection*[5]

## WEEK 2, DAY 5

# COMPASSION FATIGUE

INTEGRATION

Make a list of the ways your energy becomes depleted. Make another list of the ways that you restore your energy. Which list is longer? What does this tell you about your self-care?

Empathy is our capacity to feel the emotions of others and/or take the perspective of other people. But therein lies the trap: If we become too distressed by their suffering, we may not have the cognitive or emotional resources to help them. . . . Empathy alone can lead to burnout, but the mindfulness and care inherent in compassion foster resilience, connectedness and action.

~ Tara Brach, *Radical Compassion*[6]

# WEEK 2, DAY 6

## PRACTICING SELF-COMPASSION

INTEGRATION

Locate a large, empty bowl. Sit down and place the bowl in your lap. Look into the emptiness. Is there any part of your current situation that compares to this emptiness? Hold the empty bowl up. Open your heart with a readiness to receive what you need in order to care for yourself. Place the bowl down. Let it speak to you about your life.

Never underestimate what you can weave into your shift, work, or career to make it a healthier place for you to be. Decide that being a martyr in the workplace is a thing of the past.

~ Laura van Dernoot Lipsky and Connie Burk, *Trauma Stewardship*[7]

# WEEK 2, DAY 7

## REVIEW

INTEGRATION

Choose any or all of the following as a way to review Week Two:

- What aspects of "Welcoming Ourselves" were of greatest significance to you this past Week?

- Which Day's teaching challenged you the most? Which Day left you nodding your head yes?

- In what ways might this Week's focus on self-compassion make a difference in how you live?

- Of the quotations used this Week, which one stands out as containing the best insight for your growth in self-compassion?

- As you look back over the Week, were there moments or situations that awakened your self-compassion? Describe those times. Do they have anything in common?

- Look back over Week Two. Notice the various ways you extended compassion to yourself. List these. Read over them, and after each one, whisper, "Thank you."

- Imagine looking at yourself from a compassionate viewpoint. What would you want to say to yourself?

I used to be so afraid of my tears. I thought tears to be a sign of weakness, way too much vulnerability. But now I see these tears as my spirit's self-compassion, comforting and cleansing what aches within me, assurance that my pain is being heard and held with love.

~ Joyce Rupp (Personal Journal)

## RHYTHM

Step by step, through the forest
my feet on the pine-needled trail,
legs, muscles, tendons, nerves,
blood sails smoothly in and out.
Lungs, air, breath in, breath out,
a steady, taken-for-granted rhythm.
Each knows what to do, and does it.

Sun slowly rising, sun slowly setting,
Earth's measured rotation in space,
seasons coming, seasons going,
this rhythm, too, my life absorbs.

Ocean water carried in liberal waves,
in-out, high-low, arriving-departing,
wild storms followed by calmness,
another steady pattern teaching me.

Why then, do I allow my spirit
to be fraught with unsteady motion,
too much standing, too little sitting,
too much movement, too little stillness,
too much out and not enough in?

Teach me, Keeper of My Soul,
how to gain the steady balance,
to wed my inner rhythm with yours,
a regulated pace of tranquility.

*~ Joyce Rupp*

# THE RIVER OF SUFFERING

## REVELATION

With the spring rains long departed
the hidden sandbars come into sight.
The broad river slowly recedes,
disclosing gloomy, tan blotches
intruding upon my notion of beauty.

I long for full, flowing currents of water,
but the blue herons seem not to mind.
They find a safe perch to keep vigil
for the next meal swimming their way;
thin-legged sandpipers skitter along,
happily pecking insects on the dry sand,
while newly freed shoots of green grass
are able to finally breathe the air.

I stand on the bank of the sparse river
pondering the uneasy flow of my life
with its insistent visitation of loss,
unwelcome and unmerited suffering
seeming to bring with it nothing of worth.

But I have learned a valuable lesson—
if I cease resisting and simply allow
whatever appears in the dry shallows,
a veiled gift eventually reveals itself—
one my shuttered heart failed to recognize.

*~ Joyce Rupp*

## WEEK 3, DAY 1

## RESPONDING TO SUFFERING

INTEGRATION

What do you believe about the experience of suffering? How have your difficulties influenced the way you approach others who are suffering?

Who knows how I might have turned out if my father had lived, but through the loss of him all those years ago I think that I have learned something about how even tragedy can be a means of grace that I might never have come to any other way.

~ Frederick Buechner, "Telling Secrets"[1]

## WEEK 3, DAY 2

# THE GIFT OF EMPATHY

INTEGRATION

Recall a time when someone was able to understand what you were going through. How did their empathy affect you?

Real empathy requires that we develop the capacity to put our own concerns aside long enough to notice what someone else is going through internally, without reference to ourselves.

~ Norman Fischer, *Training in Compassion*[2]

## WEEK 3, DAY 3

# THE PATTERN OF TRANSFORMATION

INTEGRATION

What gives meaning to your life in regard to suffering? Name some insights you have gained from experiencing your own or another's suffering.

The nine months beginning in mid-1961 were perhaps the most lonely and difficult period in many ways of any that I can remember. The whole move could
appear as superficially disastrous, but it was in fact one of those creative "mis-
takes" without which there is rarely any stirring of new life.

~ Helen M. Luke, *Such Stuff as Dreams Are Made On*[3]

## WEEK 3, DAY 4

## BROKEN OPEN

INTEGRATION

In what ways have your sufferings changed you? How have they broken you open?

The acorn doesn't sprout right on the tree; it has to fall into the ground and its shell must be cracked. . . . Either you will brace, harden, and resist, or you will soften, open, and yield.

~ Cynthia Bourgeault, *The Wisdom Way of Knowing* [4]

## WEEK 3, DAY 5

## COMPASSIONATE PRESENCE

INTEGRATION

Think of a person in your life who is compassionate. This might be a relative, friend, colleague, or a historical, biblical, religious, or literary figure. What is it about this person that makes you think of him or her as a person of compassion? Imagine this person telling you about being a compassionate presence. What might he or she say?

Caregivers make effective the love of God, bending over pain and distress at a most critical moment of human life. In doing so, they embody in a beautiful and real sense the mystery of divine compassion.

~ Elizabeth A. Johnson, *Abounding in Kindness*[5]

## WEEK 3, DAY 6

# THE SHADOW SIDE OF COMPASSION

INTEGRATION

Reflect on three or four situations when you have been kind and caring in some way. What were the motivations that led to your offering compassion?

Even though the enterprises and causes I engage in may be good in themselves, if my motives for doing them are unsound, they are almost certain to turn out badly in the long run. Only that activity which is done from the Ground of the Soul . . . will have truly lasting and positive effects.

~ Cyprian Smith, O.S.B., *The Way of Paradox* [6]

# WEEK 3, DAY 7

## REVIEW

INTEGRATION

Choose any or all of the following as a way to review Week Three:

- What three aspects of "The River of Suffering" were of greatest significance to you this past Week?

- If you were to write on a tombstone an epitaph that describes your experience of suffering, what would that one-liner be?

- As you look back over the Week, did some experience or insight help to clarify how suffering might have meaning in your life?

- Draw your "River of Suffering."
  - On the river, write the perceived obstacles from the past that have caused suffering and distress in your life. Take a look at what you have placed on the river. Ask yourself: "What was my experience of these obstacles? How did they hinder the flow of my life?"
  - Then choose one of these obstacles. Reflect on what, in particular, was hurtful or stressful about this hindrance. Write these aspects next to the hindrance. Ask yourself: "When did I become free from this obstacle? How did that change for me? Did some inner growth eventually take place because of this? If so, how?"
  - Draw a boat on the river. Write or draw symbols on it for the wisdom, growth, or newness that came to you because of your experience of this obstacle.

- Of the suffering you have experienced in your life and in the lives of others, what have you found to be the most difficult in extending your compassion?

- Which Day's reflection challenged you the most? Which Day's reflection felt the most comfortable? Consider why these reflections felt so different to you.

I lifted the small brick in the flower garden, astounded to find a pale-green crocus shoot. I marveled at its urge to grow under that brick with no light, and yet the plant pushed through the ground and held on. How many humans are like that crocus, pressed down with burdens, kept in the dark captivity of anguish? They need someone to lift the brick, assure them of having room to breathe new life.

~ Joyce Rupp (Personal Journal)

## PRAYER IN A TIME OF SUFFERING

Come, Incandescent Presence,
abide by the hearth of discouragement,
fuel and revive the waning flickers of hope,
ignite the dry wick of the soul's lantern.

Float your love in on golden wings,
surround the lantern, breathe into it
until the light leaps into a strong flame,
enough to warm the winter-cold heart.

Radiant Companion of nomadic souls,
guide the way home to inner peace,
emit sparks of joy on gray-filled days,
guard unsure steps on the rocky terrain.

Let every glimmer in the midnight sky
be a welcoming beacon of confidence;
kindle the flame dimmed by suffering
into a comforting communion with you.

*~ Joyce Rupp*

# FROM HOSTILITY TO HOSPITALITY

## THIS SPLINTERED WORLD

The children of this splintered world
bear the hardships and insecurities
often fermented by impassive adults
who turn their backs on compassion.

The lives of young ones everywhere
hunger not only for food and lodging,
they ache for security and essential care,
for a love that will not abandon them.

Refugee camps, abusive foster homes,
dangerous war zones, drug-infested streets,
immigration borders—all lock them out
from the safe harbor each child deserves.

And I, what do I propose to make a change?
Am I willing to give of myself for their wellbeing?
How can the world's betrayed children survive
unless privileged people act on their behalf?

*~ Joyce Rupp*

## WEEK 4, DAY 1

# THE HAVES AND THE HAVE-NOTS

INTEGRATION

Have you ever experienced a "door" being closed to you by an individual, organization, or country? If so, what was that like for you? If you have not had this experience, how can you use your influence to help keep doors open for others?

All of us have a tendency, often without realizing it, to draw a line around what is ours. Most of the time, we see only what is within that circle and no further. Outside it, unseen and uncared for, is the rest of life: other people, other creatures, the health of Mother Earth.

~ Eknath Easwaran, *The Compassionate Universe*[1]

## WEEK 4, DAY 2

# THE TWO WOLVES IN US

INTEGRATION

Recall the story told by the grandmother on page 108 in *Boundless Compassion* in which she describes the two wolves fighting within her. When asked if the wolf of love or the wolf of hate would win, she wisely responded that it would depend on the one that she chose to feed. How do you experience these two wolves within yourself?

The wolf of love sees a vast horizon, with all beings included in the circle of "us."
That circle shrinks down for the wolf of hate, so that only the nation, or tribe,
or friends and family—or, in the extreme, only the individual self—is held as
"us," surrounded by the threatening masses of "them."

~ Rick Hanson, *Buddha's Brain*[2]

## WEEK 4, DAY 3

## FAR FROM THE TREE

INTEGRATION

What would you name as your weaknesses and vulnerabilities? How do these affect your approach and attitude toward people with disabilities or other differences whom society avoids?

There is something ironic in prejudice against the disabled and their families, because their plight might befall anybody. Straight men are unlikely to wake up gay one morning, and white children don't become black; but any of us could be disabled in an instant.

~ Andrew Solomon, *Far From the Tree*[3]

## WEEK 4, DAY 4

## REMOVING THE BOULDERS

INTEGRATION

What are some of the "boulders" in your life that keep you from actively working for greater justice regarding those who are oppressed? How might you remove them?

It is true enough that we could make this world more just, equal, and peaceful, but something holds us back, in all our complicated fear and human hesitation. It's sometimes just plain hard to locate the will to be in kinship even though, at the same time, it's our deepest longing.

~ Gregory Boyle, *Barking to the Choir*[4]

## WEEK 4, DAY 5

## CULTIVATING RELATIONSHIPS

INTEGRATION

What do you most enjoy about your relationships with persons to whom you extend compassion? What do you find most difficult or challenging in a relationship that focuses on being compassionate?

A young woman from Romania thanked me for a scarf I had wrapped and given her on her birthday. She said, "No one has ever given me a present before. I never had a birthday until I met you."

~ Mary Pipher, *The Middle of Everywhere*[5]

## WEEK 4, DAY 6

## HAVE YOU LOVED WELL?

INTEGRATION

The Works of Compassion come from Matthew 25:35–36: "I was hungry and you gave me food, I was thirsty and you gave me something to drink, I was a stranger and you welcomed me, I was naked and you gave me clothing, I was sick and you took care of me, I was in prison and you visited me." Which of the Works of Compassion most reflects your compassionate actions? Which one least reflects your compassionate actions? What part of Matthew 25 invites you to engage more fully with compassionate action?

Compassion is of little value if it remains an idea. It must become our attitude toward others, reflected in all our thoughts and actions.

~ The Dalai Lama, *An Open Heart*[6]

# WEEK 4, DAY 7

## REVIEW

INTEGRATION

Choose any or all of the following as a way to review Week Four:

- What three aspects of "From Hostility to Hospitality" were of greatest significance to you this past Week?

- As you look back over the Week, what were the insights or examples that awakened a fuller understanding for you of what it means to be marginalized?

- What stands out for you as most helpful in lessening the great divide between the haves and the have-nots?

- Draw a circle. On the outer edge of the circle write the names of individuals and groups whom you tend to marginalize. Then, slowly, intentionally, and prayerfully, write your name next to any of the names that you are willing to join there on the margin. What is one concrete action you could take to join them?

- Browse through the daily news. Pause by each story of someone, or some group, who experiences marginalization. What do you think and how do you feel about this person or group? What would it be like if you opened your heart and welcomed any or all of these persons whose stories you are reading?

- Reflect on how you lived this Week. What are some ways that you "loved well" through one or more of the Works of Compassion?

I long to grow in being aware of the message in Matthew 25:35–36—that every person who comes into my life bears the presence of divinity. As much as I desire this to be the inspiration and foundation of my compassionate living, it all too quickly slips from my consciousness.

~ Joyce Rupp (Personal Journal)

# WHAT I DO TO OTHERS

Indwelling Presence,
when I insist on wrapping my arms
tightly around my small circle of life,
free them to open and stretch forth
with generous concern for others.

When I get too ensnared in myself
and only intent on personal desires,
move me beyond self-indulgence
to join with people on the margins.

When I deliberately turn my attention
away from the existence of suffering,
resurrect my innate ability to be caring
until I move toward other people's pain.

When I proceed to walk unmoved
past wounded ones on life's pathway,
draw forth my compassionate courage
so I will choose to stop and assist.

When I forget (as you know I often do),
remind me that whatsoever I do to others
I am doing to you, the Holy Essence,
dwelling in each and every one on the way.

*~ Joyce Rupp*

# A THOUSAND UNBREAKABLE LINKS

## STOMP

The big boot coming down
on the dying bumblebee,
the deliberate stomp
on top of the helpless insect
unable to move.
I stared in disbelief, felt horror
at the sound of the crunch,
my pain going to all creatures
treated carelessly by those
indifferent to their pain.

He noticed the look on my face,
"I shouldn't have done that,
should I?"

I said nothing, too grieved to reply.

*~ Joyce Rupp*

# WEEK 5, DAY 1

## LIVING ON PLANET EARTH

INTEGRATION

Imagine you are an astronaut looking out into space, viewing our home planet, Earth. What are the benefits and gifts from your having lived on this planet? What would life be like for you if you could not return? What part of nature would you miss the most? After considering these questions, create a list of what you value most about being a citizen of Earth.

We are all members of the earth family, interconnected through the planet's fragile web of life. We all have a duty to live in a manner that protects the earth's ecological processes, and the rights and welfare of all species and all people.

~ Vandana Shiva, *Earth Democracy*[1]

## WEEK 5, DAY 2

## DIFFERENT THAN, NOT BETTER THAN

INTEGRATION

What part of creation do you find most difficult to consider being your sister or brother? When did this attitude or idea develop in you? What would it take for you to change your mental or emotional response?

Nothing is itself in any adequate manner without everything else. Humans are an abstraction if we think of ourselves separate from the air and the water and the sunshine and the earth under our feet. If we exploit and diminish the earth, we exploit and diminish our own being.

~ Jay B. McDaniel, *Earth, Sky, Gods and Mortals*[2]

## WEEK 5, DAY 3

# ALL CREATION GROANS

INTEGRATION

Visualize your favorite flower, food, and animal. How would you feel if any of these no longer existed? What if a special place in nature that you enjoy was destroyed? Describe what your life might be like if that place and similar ones no longer existed anywhere on Earth.

Until we can grieve for our planet and its future inhabitants, we cannot fully feel or enact our love for them. Such grief is frequently suppressed, not only because it is socially awkward. It is also denied because it is both painful and hard to believe.

~ Joanna Macy, *World as Lover, World as Self*[3]

## WEEK 5, DAY 4

## NATURE AS "THOU"

INTEGRATION

If you have ever entered into a "thou" relationship—a personal, intimate relationship—with nature, describe this experience. How does it compare with a relationship you have with someone you love? If there is a part of you that resists relating to nature as a "thou," what causes this to be so?

The first way of seeing with the physical eye shows a world of fact. The second seeing is a beholding with the eye of the soul that reveals a world of meaning. With the second there is an inner deepening of our relationship with the tree.

~ Carolyn W. Toben, *Recovering a Sense of the Sacred*[4]

# WEEK 5, DAY 5

## THINKING LIKE A MOUNTAIN

INTEGRATION

Select a scenario of suffering, such as a destroyed rainforest, polluted river, young albatross dying from eating plastic, mountainside gouged out by mining, elephant killed for its tusks, or prairie flower becoming extinct, or choose another part of creation that has entered your awareness. Write a letter to this suffering part of Earth.

The mending of the world means pressing our ear to the land to hear the heart-beat of the Mother, learning to read her pulses, diagnose her ailments, intuit healing remedies. It means slowing down enough to let the pain of the world all the way into our hearts, allowing our hearts to break open, and acting from that broken-open space.

~ Mirabai Starr, *Wild Mercy* [5]

## WEEK 5, DAY 6

# CARING FOR EARTH

INTEGRATION

What is one deliberate action you can take to maintain the health and heal the wounds of our planet? How might you go about this action? Is there anything you fear, resist, or consider especially difficult in attempting to do this?

Each community can take from the bounty of the earth whatever it needs for subsistence, but it also has the duty to protect the earth and to ensure its fruitfulness for coming generations.

~ Pope Francis, *Laudato Si'*[6]

# WEEK 5, DAY 7

## REVIEW

INTEGRATION

Choose any or all of the following as a way to review Week Five:

- What three aspects of "A Thousand Unbreakable Links" were of greatest significance to you this past Week?

- In what way has this Week's study led you to a keener sense of your interdependence with all that exists?

- As you look back over Week Five, what particular moments or situations awakened you to both the beauty and the wounds of creation?

- Take an hour to be with some form of nonhuman life: animals, plants, birds, and so on. Observe with your senses. Get to know what you are observing as a "thou." Keep your own interests and thoughts out of the way. Be present as a companion in a caring relationship. Then afterward consider what you learned or experienced during your time of companionship.

- As you look over the Week, did you notice any part of creation's suffering that you had not been aware of in the past? How did that affect you?

- Which Day's reflection challenged you the most? Which one left you nodding your head yes?

- List the ways you have observed the suffering of creation during the past Week. Write a psalm of lament in Earth's voice.

*Walking yesterday on the bike trail. A family with two young girls. We stopped by a bench to look onto the river. A small spider was on the bottom of the wooden railing. The little girl screamed, "Spider! Ack!," then quickly lifted up her foot and smashed the spider. Her father said weakly, "You shouldn't kill spiders. They're good. They eat other bugs." She snapped, "I don't care. I don't like it."*

~ Joyce Rupp (Personal Journal)

## ECHOES OF LAUGHTER

Thank you, Ingenious Spirit, abiding among
all that rests and dreams, leaps and crawls,
swims and hops, plays and runs wildly,
hides away snugly and stands up boldly.

Echoes of laughter spill out through creation,
carrying their sounds in squeaking mice,
giddy neighs of yearlings in the pasture,
the cawing of raucous crows on tree tops.

Brooks giggle when carried between stones,
aspen branches laugh as the breeze lifts them,
glaciers crack jokes in spite of their frozen breath,
and humpback whales smile as they sing to another.

Earthworms wiggle joyfully through compost,
spider monkeys leap happily from tree to tree,
rice paddies sway with breathy sighs of gladness
and the vast oceans splash their dancing waves.

Everywhere laughter fills the land and water,
a steady mirth moves through forest and city,
joyous sounds to gladden the human heart,
gifts from you, Music Maker of Earth's melodies.

*~ Joyce Rupp*

# BECOMING A COMPASSIONATE PRESENCE

## MENTORS OF COMPASSION

They lived among us,
durable as redwood trees
thriving in ancient forests.
Personalities and lifestyles,
valued qualities, teachings
we eagerly imbibed,
and sometimes envied,
for their brave divergence
from our tightly held beliefs.

Most often, we were drawn
toward their fragrance of goodness,
an unnamed essence of kindness
wafting through our encounters
with their compassionate lives.

Today the names of the deceased,
those kindhearted ones I admire,
tumble forth from my memory,
gifting me with how I want to live,
reminding me of how I, too,
can be a carrier of great love,
living like these courageous souls
forever abiding in my heart.

*~ Joyce Rupp*

# WEEK 6, DAY 1

## OUR COMMON HUMANITY

INTEGRATION

What does "our common humanity" mean to you in your practice of compassion? Describe several experiences when this concept has influenced your life.

When our troubled, painful experiences are framed by the recognition that countless others have undergone similar hardships, the blow is softened. The pain still hurts, but it doesn't become compounded by feelings of separation.

~ Kristen Neff, *Self-Compassion*[1]

## WEEK 6, DAY 2

# HOW SCIENCE BENEFITS COMPASSION

INTEGRATION

How are you contributing to the strength of a morphogenic field—a region of energy within and around a people carrying information, habits, and memories that contribute to change—by your repeated patterns of compassionate thoughts and actions?

We know we are beings of light and energy who form morphogenic fields that create possibilities for others. . . . This is our moment. Let us live connected and in love, so that generations to come will look at us and say, "They were the first generations to really get it."

~ Judy Cannato, *Radical Amazement*[2]

## WEEK 6, DAY 3

# PAYING THE PRICE

INTEGRATION

What do you most fear in "paying the price" for being compassionate?

The more divine love can shine through the core of our lives, the freer we are to overcome the impasses we find ourselves in. . . . Our challenge today is to stay the course of love in a world that resists love, fears love, and rejects the cost of love.

~ Ilia Delio, *The Unbearable Wholeness of Being*[3]

# WEEK 6, DAY 4

## ONE GOOD DEED

### INTEGRATION

Look back on your life. Find one good deed of yours that made a difference. Describe how this happened and what it was like for you to do this.

I suspect that the most basic and powerful way to connect to another person is to listen. Just listen. Perhaps the most important thing we ever give each other is our attention. And especially if it's given from the heart.

~ Rachel Naomi Remen, M.D., *Kitchen Table Wisdom*[4]

## WEEK 6, DAY 5

## MENTORS OF COMPASSION

INTEGRATION

Who are your mentors of compassion? How have they inspired you?

We become part of a lineage of people who have cultivated their bravery through-out history, people who, against enormous odds, have stayed open to great diffi-culties and painful situations and transformed them into the path of awakening.

~ Pema Chödrön, *Start Where You Are*[5]

# WEEK 6, DAY 6

## CARRYING HOPE IN OUR HEARTS

INTEGRATION

Where do you find hope in your life and in the life of our world?
How do you maintain hope in difficult times?

Hope . . . is not the same as joy that things are going well, or willingness to invest in enterprises that are obviously headed for early success, but rather an ability to work for something because it is good, not just because it stands a chance to succeed.

~ Václav Havel, *Disturbing the Peace*[6]

## WEEK 6, DAY 7

## REVIEW

INTEGRATION

Choose any or all of the following as a way to review Week Six:

- What three aspects of "Becoming a Compassionate Presence" were of greatest significance to you this past Week?

- What would you name as the central characteristic of a "compassionate presence"?

- Name the choices you intend to make regarding the suffering of self and the suffering of all beings, both human and nonhuman.

- Of the quotations used this Week, which one stands out as containing the best insight for becoming a compassionate presence?

- Which Day's reflection challenged you the most? Which Day's reflection felt the most comfortable? Consider why these reflections felt so different to you.

- How can you be a compassionate presence in a world where violence and poverty seem endless?

- As you complete this last review, take a wide sweep over the past six Weeks. Reflect on what you want to remember. Recall how you felt drawn at certain times toward a particular change in attitude or behavior. Which of the Weeks most stimulated your interest and led you to want to become more compassionate?

*My heart brims over with gratitude when I think of how much I have received from others when I was in need of compassion. I want to share what I have received, give without hesitation or self-pity, bring this bounty to the emptied cup of another, pour freely from the abundance of my heart.*

~ Joyce Rupp (Personal Journal)

## AN INSTRUMENT OF COMPASSION

When the world is sunk in sleep
and the heavens are ink-dark
who is it that pulls so mightily
on the strings of my heart?

~ Rabindranath Tagore[7]


A musical instrument, destined to contribute,
offers itself without reserve to the player,
allows the touch of its yielded strings
to vibrate in the heart of those who receive.

I go forth willingly to be the heart-strings,
ready to be an instrument of your divine love,
grateful to carry the harmony of compassion,
conveying the message of hope and resilience.

Source of Songs reverberating everywhere,
strumming loving music upon human hearts,
revive my compassion in the midnight hours
and float this love freely in the active hours of day.

*~ Joyce Rupp*

# EPILOGUE

## MAGNETS OF COMPASSION

Life moves swiftly. When constant diversions distract us, we tend to lose what has captured our attention and enthused our hearts. This has happened when I've read a book that kindled my enthusiasm or when I departed from an energizing retreat filled with renewed zest for spiritual growth. As the weeks and months went by, that passion dissipated and eventually fell to the wayside. I've gradually learned to avoid this disintegrating process by deliberately engaging with what urges me toward further growth.

You can avoid losing your desire to be a compassionate presence by reengaging with *The Boundless Compassion Journal* when you find your motivation or your active compassion waning. For example: If you forget about offering compassion to yourself, go back to that section and read what surfaced for you. If you find yourself struggling with irritation regarding another person, return to Week One and review the insights and awareness that came alive for you. When you feel emotionally overwrought with the heartaches of someone you love, look at Week Three and recall what you learned about suffering and how to approach compassionate caring.

A valuable aid to remaining faithful to compassionate living is by associating with others who have a similar focus and desire. In *Boundless Compassion* I suggest forming a monthly "Circle of Compassion" to foster kinship, along with ongoing learning and inspiration (cf. pp. 9–10). If you do not already belong to such a group, please consider initiating one. Take a deep breath of trust, gather other persons who share your heart's vision, and step forth on a new and valuable venture.

Another way of keeping compassion alive is by setting a daily intention to be a *magnet of compassion*. In Macrina Wiederkehr's book *Abide*, she refers to an oft-quoted line in which God speaks to the mystic Mechtild of Magdeburg: "I will draw my breath and your soul will come to me like a needle to a magnet."[1] The main attribute of a magnet exists in its ability to attract. This magnetic field is invisible but the consequences of its drawing power are revealed in its action. The stronger the magnetic field, the greater the magnet's drawing power. You have a powerful, attracting ability within you—the magnetic field of compassion. And you have the Holy One's unending love enticing this quality to come forth from you.

What if you dedicated yourself to being a magnet of compassion, day after day, week after week? Imagine how the world around you could be drawn toward greater justice, respect and kindness. Imagine the intense pull toward loving-kindness that would touch the suffering in our world.

On the concluding page of Christina Feldman's *Boundless Heart*, she writes, "There is no higher motivation or intention in this life than to have compassion, with its dimension of empathy and responsiveness, at the heart of all we do."[2] This is possible. I believe it with all my heart. This conviction keeps my hope alive. Let us join together and be generous with our loving presence. Let us be magnets of compassion.

~ Joyce Rupp

# APPENDIX

## WEEKLY REFLECTION WITH GROUPS

At the opening of each Week's Boundless Compassion gathering, a bell or gong is sounded and/or a candle is lit to call the group into a brief time of silence. A check in time follows this, with those present describing in a few sentences the interior atmosphere they are bringing to the conversation—the mental and emotional disposition, the inner climate of mind and heart.

The following questions can then be used for reflection on the past week's journaling. Good listening skills, such as waiting until all have a chance to speak before proceeding to speak again, will be assumed to be a part of this time of sharing.

1. As you reflect on your journaling experience this Week, what title would you give to it? What leads you to choose this title?
2. Did anything in particular surprise you in what came forth?
3. Which prompt most drew you to want to journal?
4. Were any difficulties encountered due to the content or the journaling process?
5. Have any unresolved issues been raised regarding the Week's topic?
6. Which Day was your most enjoyable?
7. Which Day held the clearest insight?

8. What did you find most challenging for this Week?
9. Is there something that continues to stir your curiosity?
10. Is there anything else you would like to mention about your Week of journaling?

Before closing, those present are invited (but not obliged) to read one of their journal entries from the week. The group pauses after each reading for a brief silence to honor what was shared. No discussion follows.

Close with a selection from *Prayers of Boundless Compassion* or choose another option that fits with the theme of that week.

# NOTES

## INTRODUCTION

1. Catherine T. Nerney, *The Compassion Connection: Recovering Our Original Oneness* (Maryknoll, NY: Orbis Books, 2018), 43.

2. Rabindranath Tagore, "The Problem of Self," in *The Essential Tagore*, eds. Fakrul Alam and Radha Chakravarty  (Cambridge, MA: Belknap Press, 2014), 165.

## WEEK ONE: COMPASSION AS A WAY OF LIFE

1. "The Charter for Compassion," charterforcompassion.org/charter/affirm.

2. Macrina Wiederkehr, *The Song of the Seed: A Monastic Way of Tending the Soul* (San Francisco: Harper San Francisco, 1997), 8.

3. Paul Gilbert, *The Compassionate Mind: How to Use Compassion to Develop Happiness, Self-Acceptance, and Wellbeing* (London: Constable and Robinson, 2009), 54.

4. Parker J. Palmer, *An Undivided Life: Seeking Wholeness in Ourselves, Our Work, and Our World,* read by the author (Sounds True, 2009), audiobook, 5 hrs., 31 min.

5. Piero Ferrucci, *The Power of Kindness: The Unexpected Benefits of Leading a Compassionate Life* (New York: TarcherPerigee, 2006), 47.

6. Elaine Prevallet, *Toward a Spirituality for Global Justice: A Call to Kinship* (Louisville, KY: Sowers Books and Videos, 2005), 54.

## WEEK TWO: WELCOMING OURSELVES

1. Tara Brach, *Radical Compassion: Learning to Love Yourself and Your World with the Practice of RAIN* (New York: Viking, 2019), 125.

2. Robert J. Wicks, *Night Call: Embracing Compassion and Hope in a Troubled World* (Oxford: Oxford University Press, 2017), 93.

3. Matthew Fox, *Meditations with Meister Eckhart* (Rochester, VT: Bear and Company, 1983), 111.

4. Diane M. Millis, *Re-Creating a Life: Learning How to Tell Our Most Life-Giving Story* (Bellevue, WA: SDI Press, 2019), 145.

5. Brené Brown, *The Gifts of Imperfection: Let Go of Who You Think You're Supposed to Be and Embrace Who You Are* (Center City, MN: Hazelden Publishing, 2010), 56–57.

6. Brach, *Radical Compassion*, 212.

7. Laura van Dernoot Lipsky with Connie Burk, *Trauma Stewardship: An Everyday Guide to Caring for Self While Caring for Others* (San Francisco: Berrett-Koehler Publishers, 2009), 211.

## WEEK THREE: THE RIVER OF SUFFERING

1. Frederick Buechner, "Telling Secrets," in Diane M. Millis, *Re-Creating a Life: Learning How to Tell Our Most Life-Giving Story* (Bellevue, WA: SDI Press, 2019), 165.

2. Norman Fischer, *Training in Compassion: Zen Teachings on the Practice of Lojong* (Boston: Shambhala, 2013), 11.

3. Helen M. Luke, *Such Stuff as Dreams Are Made On: The Autobiography and Journals of Helen M. Luke* (New York: Harmony / Bell Tower, 2001), 71.

4. Cynthia Bourgeault, *The Wisdom Way of Knowing: Reclaiming an Ancient Tradition to Awaken the Heart* (San Francisco: Jossey-Bass, 2003), 67, 75.

5. Elizabeth A. Johnson, *Abounding in Kindness: Writing for the People of God* (Maryknoll, NY: Orbis Books, 2015), 154.

6. Cyprian Smith, O.S.B., *The Way of Paradox: Spiritual Life as Taught by Meister Eckhart* (London: Darton, Longman, and Todd, 2004), 115.

## WEEK FOUR: FROM HOSTILITY TO HOSPITALITY

1. Eknath Easwaran, *The Compassionate Universe: The Power of the Individual to Heal the Environment* (Tomales, CA: Nilgiri Press, 1993), 135.

2. Rick Hanson, *Buddha's Brain: The Practical Neuroscience of Happiness, Love, and Wisdom* (Oakland, CA: New Harbinger Publications, 2009), 131.

3. Andrew Solomon, *Far From the Tree: Parents, Children and the Search for Identity* (New York: Scribner, 2012), 22.

4. Gregory Boyle, *Barking to the Choir: The Power of Radical Kinship* (New York: Simon and Schuster, 2017), 202.

5. Mary Pipher, *The Middle of Everywhere: Helping Refugees Enter the American Community* (New York: Harcourt, 2003), 17.

6. The Dalai Lama, *An Open Heart: Practicing Compassion in Everyday Life* (New York: Back Bay Books, 2002), 48.

## WEEK FIVE: A THOUSAND UNBREAKABLE LINKS

1. Vandana Shiva, *Earth Democracy: Justice, Sustainability, and Peace* (Berkeley, CA: North Atlantic Books, 2015), 9.

2. Jay B. McDaniel, *Earth, Sky, Gods and Mortals: Developing an Ecological Spirituality* (Eugene, OR: Wipf and Stock Publishers, 2009), vii.

3. Joanna Macy, *World as Lover, World as Self: Courage for Global Justice and Ecological Renewal* (Berkeley, CA: Parallax Press, 2003), 20.

4. Carolyn W. Toben, *Recovering a Sense of the Sacred: Conversations with Thomas Berry* (Whitsett, NC: Timberlake Earth Sanctuary Press, 2012), 83.

5. Mirabai Starr, *Wild Mercy: Living the Fierce and Tender Wisdom of the Women Mystics* (Boulder, CO: Sounds True, 2019), 138–39.

6. Francis, *Laudato Si'*, encyclical letter, Vatican website, May 24, 2015, sec. 67, www.vatican.va/content/francesco/en/encyclicals/documents/papa-francesco_20150524_enciclica-laudato-si.html.

## WEEK SIX: BECOMING A COMPASSIONATE PRESENCE

1. Kristen Neff, *Self-Compassion: The Proven Power of Being Kind to Yourself* (New York: William Morrow Paperbacks, 2015), 65.

2. Judy Cannato, *Radical Amazement: Contemplative Lessons from Black Holes, Supernovas, and Other Wonders of the Universe* (Notre Dame, IN: Ave Maria Press, 2006), 144.

3. Ilia Delio, *The Unbearable Wholeness of Being: God, Evolution, and the Power of Love* (Maryknoll, NY: Orbis Books, 2013), 197.

4. Rachel Naomi Remen, M.D., *Kitchen Table Wisdom: Stories that Heal* (New York: Riverhead Books, 2006), 143.

5. Pema Chödrön, *Start Where You Are: A Guide to Compassionate Living* (Boulder, CO: Shambhala Publications, 2018), 49.

6. Václav Havel, *Disturbing the Peace: A Conversation with Karel Huizdala* (New York: Vintage Books, 1991), 181–82.

7. Rabindranath Tagore, "An Instrument of Compassion," in *Show Yourself to My Soul*, trans. James Talarovic (Notre Dame, IN: Sorin Books, 2002), 82.

## EPILOGUE

1. Macrina Wiederkehr, *Abide: Keeping Vigil with the Word of God* (Collegeville, MN: Liturgical Press, 2011), 49.

2. Christina Feldman, *Boundless Heart: The Buddha's Path of Kindness, Compassion, Joy, and Equanimity* (Boulder, CO: Shambhala Publications, 2017), 144.

*Joyce Rupp* is well known for her work as a writer, spiritual midwife, international retreat leader, and conference speaker. Her book *Boundless Compassion* was named one of the Top 50 Spirituality Books of 2018 by Spirituality and Practice and earned awards from both the Catholic Press Association (first place) and the Association of Catholic Publishers (second place). She is the author of numerous bestselling books, including *Prayers of Boundless Compassion, Praying Our Goodbyes, Open the Door, Fragments of Your Ancient Name,* and *Prayers of Boundless Compassion.*

Rupp is a member of the Servite (Servants of Mary) community. She is a consultant and resource person for the Boundless Compassion program's certified facilitators. She lives in West Des Moines, Iowa.

www.joycerupp.com
Facebook: @joycerupp

Servite Center of Compassion: www.osms.org/servite-center-of-compassion

# MORE RESOURCES FOR
# BOUNDLESS COMPASSION

The definitive Christian guide to compassion, *Boundless Compassion* is the culmination of Joyce Rupp's research and work as codirector of the Servite Institute of Compassionate Presence.

Through this six-week personal transformation process for developing and deepening compassion, Rupp nudges, encourages, and inspires you to grow in the kind of love that motivated Jesus' life and his mission for his disciples.

These DVDs, as well as digital downloads of the videos, can only be purchased from the gift shop at **osms.org**.

## "The most significant prayer experience you'll have this year or for years to come."
### —Robert J. Wicks
Author of *Riding the Dragon*

Compassion was the center of Jesus' ministry and his mission for his disciples—and his call for us today. With forty original prayers, blessings, and meditations, Joyce Rupp gives you the words to develop compassion in yourself as never before and to reenergize your ability to offer loving kindness to those around you.